Steve's
A to Z of
Sport

Iain Welch

D1208744

This book is dedicated to Angharad, my family
and my friends.

Thank you for everything.
I could not have done this without you.

Printed in Great Britain by Orphans Press.
orphans.co.uk

Copyright © Iain Welch
Iain Welch asserts the right to be identified as the author of this work. He does this in
accordance with the Copyright, Designs and Patents act 1988. No part of this book may
be copied, shared, transmitted, resold or reproduced without prior permission.

All rights reserved.

This edition printed in 2017

Aa is for Archery, Athletics and Aqua Aerobics

Bb is for Badminton, Baseball and Bowling

Cc is for Cricket, Caber Tossing and Climbing

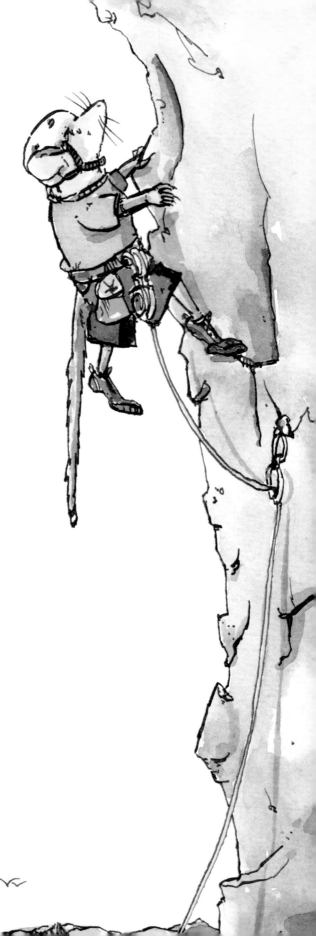

Dd is for Diving, Discus and Downhill Skiing

Ee is for Endurance Running

Also, for Eating a Healthy Snack!

F f is for Fencing, Football and Figure Skating.

G g is for
Go Karting,
Gymnastics
and Golf

Hh is for High Jumping, High Diving and Hockey

Ii is for
Ice Hockey,
Inline Skating
and Ice Climbing

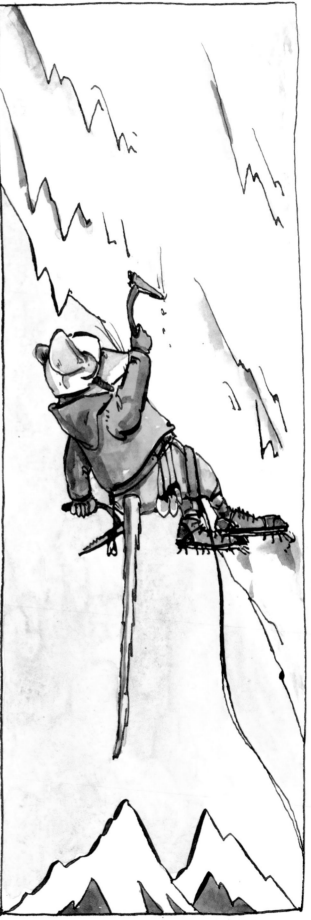

Jj is for Jet Skiing, Javelin and Judo

K k is for
Keirin,
Kayaking
and
Kitesurfing

Ll is for
Long Jumping, Lacrosse and Lawn Bowls

Mm is for
Mini Golf,
Marathon Running
and
Mountain Biking

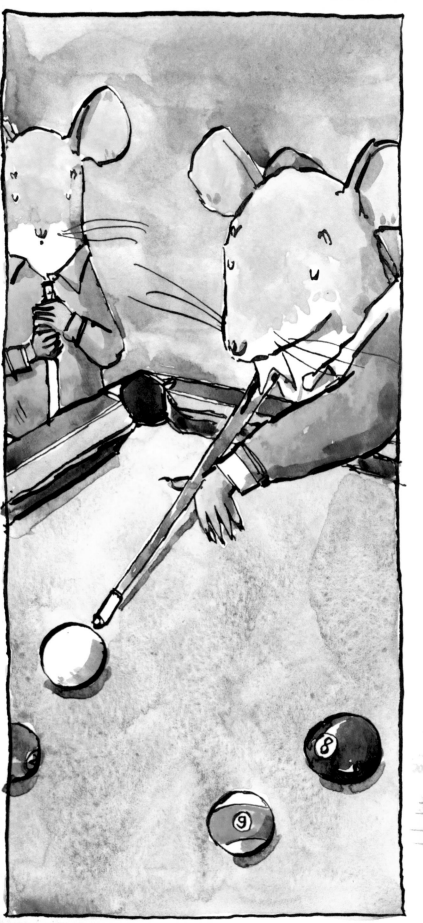

N n is
for
Netball
and Nine
Ball Pool

O o is for
Orienteering
and
Offroading

P p is for
Pole Vaulting, Paragliding and Paddleboarding

Q q is
for Quoits
and for
Quadbiking

Rr is for
Roller Derby,
Rugby and
Rowing

S s is for
Swimming,
Skateboarding
and
Snowboarding

Tt is for Table Tennis, Tabogganing and Tai Chi

U u is for
Unicycling
and for
Underwater
Hockey

V v is for
Volleyball
and for
Vaulting

W w is for Windsurfing, Wheelchair Rugby and Wrestling

X x is for X-Country

Y y is for Yoga

Zz is for....